CLASSIC FLORIDA STYLE

THE HOUSES OF TAYLOR & TAYLOR

CLASSIC
FLORIDA STYLE
THE HOUSES OF TAYLOR & TAYLOR

WRITTEN WITH BETH DUNLOP
PHOTOGRAPHY BY DEBORAH WHITLAW LLEWELLYN

THE MONACELLI PRESS

To our parents, Bette and Laurie Taylor
and Helen and Joseph Israel,
who nurtured our talents and appreciation for Florida
when they were here with us . . .
and who continue to do so in our hearts every day.

Copyright © 2014 by The Monacelli Press, LLC.

All rights reserved.
Published in the United States in 2014 by The Monacelli Press, LLC.

Library of Congress Control Number: 2013953820

Photograph page 44: Daniel Gomez

Printed in China

www.monacellipress.com

10 9 8 7 6 5 4 3 2 1
First edition

Designed by Doug Turshen with Steve Turner

contents

preface

They say that opposites attract, and we are certainly proof that it's true. William is a fifth-generation Floridian and I'm a New Yorker. William loves to immerse himself in history, while I live much more in the moment. William was swimming almost before he could walk; he loves being at the beach and in or on the ocean or almost any body of water. I love to look at the beach, to walk on it, to admire its beauty and tranquility, but I have a life-long fear of the water. And those differences are just the beginning.

Yet our firm, Taylor & Taylor, was born of a personal and professional union that has now lasted well over thirty years. William is an architect and I'm an interior designer, and we've established ways of working that help our individual designs mesh quite seamlessly with each other. We met at the University of Florida, married, ultimately settled in Miami Beach, had two children, opened our office in a quaint little Spanish bungalow, and since then have shared our vision with dozens of clients.

We believe that Florida is not only a state but a state of mind—especially as reflected in design. It's a land infused with character, class, color, texture, pattern, light, and much more. It's no accident that it is called the Sunshine State. We also believe that Florida's design has too often gotten a bad rap—for being too trendy, too kitschy, too ephemeral. We like to think that our work puts those notions to rest. We are both avid readers and explorers of architectural and design history, and we delve deep into history to find forms that help our projects express a sense of the past and a sense of place but that provide a connection to the present as well. We look closely at the land and the landscape to derive forms for our buildings and to find color, pattern, and texture for the interiors. We also search the world over for furniture, textiles, fittings, and ornaments. We consider our most successful projects those where we can bring our knowledge of history, contemporary design, and decorative arts to bear as we fill the rooms of our clients' houses.

We know Florida and are intimately aware of its subtleties, which others can miss. And from subtlety comes sophistication. For us, Florida also means the whole experience of living indoors as well as out, so we purposefully blur the boundaries between the two to create strong connections between the built environment and nature. To us, that is the Florida experience that everyone should have.

Most of us have a nostalgic connection to the past, but we acknowledge that what we really want is to live a modern life in a romanticized notion of the past. That's what we provide: a way for this to happen gracefully. As William often tells clients, one of the first times he saw a house that meant something profound to him was when his father took him to see the house his great-grandfather had built, in eastern Hillsborough County, near Tampa. It was just two pavilions connected by a veranda, and his great-grandmother had split the shingles for it. He never forgot it, its simplicity, or how even such a humble structure had provided everything they needed.

The houses we design, being modern, are often big, but we are careful never to let them overpower the site. We look for ways to let light and air in—via courtyards, loggias, outdoor living rooms, windows—and to connect space to place. This is true even when we are only responsible for a project's interior architecture. Though we often do projects together where we serve as both the architect and interior designer, we also frequently work with other architects or renovate an existing residence.

Because of our fascination with historic elements, we have become known for our ability to interpret historic architecture in ways that meet the needs of modern codes and modern lifestyles. We particularly love the array of architectural styles found in the Caribbean and the Southwest: British Colonial, Caribbean Regency, Mission, Spanish Colonial Revival. But we also love the historic architecture of Florida itself, from Mediterranean to Art Deco. The ways in which these earlier styles meshed the rustic and romantic are fascinating to us still, after all these years of looking and learning. That blend has become our best-known stylistic motif, whether we are reinterpreting and drawing inspiration from the architecture of Bermuda, the homes of Santa Barbara's George Washington Smith, or the haciendas of San Miguel de Allende.

Our interior aesthetic is less easily defined—because we work with our clients and their own personal sense of style—but we have powerful guiding principals. First, we believe that a house must have an intuitive flow that causes you to walk through every room every day. Houses are meant to be lived in fully; each day, as you pass through the rooms of your house, you should feel enriched. We also believe starting with beautiful and well-proportioned spaces makes a difference.

We pay particular attention to the treatments of floors and walls, for example, to enhance a room's mood. I confess that I have a particular fondness for using unexpected wall coverings of grass cloth or silk. I also have worked to train my eye—not just for furniture, but for color and texture, for pattern and placement. As William and I explore the world, we always keep in mind how what we see could be interpreted in the rooms we design. Any given project represents knowledge and objects gleaned from years of our travels and shopping. I find objects and objects find me. I believe a room has to be beautiful when it's empty—and should only get better when you start putting things in it. I look everywhere, from the finest of antiques shops in Europe to junk shops down the street. I've found terrific chairs sitting on a sidewalk that were being tossed out. When a piece is good, it's good, no matter where it comes from.

Together, we have developed a style that is at once refined and exuberant—let us not forget that we *are* in Florida! Our work uses Florida as an ingredient, celebrating all that is special about it, from the climate and the very bright sunlight to the flora and fauna. We draw on our knowledge of architectural and design history and the decorative arts as a base, and then tweak the elements we decide to incorporate to make them more tropical, more relaxed. And yet we keep our work classical, too. To us, it's all in how you process ideas. We look at Florida through a very particular lens, and we love what we see. We can take a photograph of a flamingo and not only make it fine art, but use it as the jumping-off point for an entire design palette. We can look at an allée of palm trees or the sand and shells on the beach and derive inspiration from them. We count ourselves lucky to live in a place that is filled with so much natural beauty and so much joy. Our work, we hope, shows that spirit.

—*Phyllis Taylor*

nautical

The very definition of a place to escape, this house on a private island near Key West is accessible only by private launch with access from a private beach. It's a two-story, Key West–style cottage with clapboard siding, gingerbread ornament, and mahogany trim. We were asked to renovate the existing house and make it brighter and more open.

The first architectural intervention was to remove a light-blocking staircase and to replace it with one that could accommodate a Palladian window—a breath of light and air. This semicircular stair hall was the key to bringing the profuse Florida sunlight into the house, which had previously been just too dark.

We created a checkerboard of gray and white marble on the floors to give the cottage a certain Southern formality that is part Charleston and part Key West. The owners of the house had tired of "Key West Casual," which challenged us to think quite creatively. For example, the walls are covered in an acid-green grass cloth. The color, as Phyllis put it, "is like biting into a lime: you've got the pucker, but it is still refreshing."

In fact, all the colors we chose reinforce the location—and it is such a nice setting. The lime green and lemon yellow, sky blue and sea aqua set against white millwork make it all very sunny and beach-worthy,

without losing a sense of sophistication. The living room carpet is basically styled *à la chinois*, as if a ship's captain could have brought it back from his spice trade voyages, but then again it's got a little bit of a fisherman-knit sweater to it, too!

The living room sofa is surprisingly covered in velvet—practically unheard of in Key West—but we opted for a light, beautiful aqua blue so it still speaks of the tropics. Another twist is the all-white, mounted marlin in the den. We got it from a taxidermist before the realistic colors were put back on it, thus making it more of a piece of sculpture than a fishing trophy. Another nautical touch comes from the semaphore flags we found in an antiques shop in Sandwich, on Cape Cod, which we framed to enhance the boy's room.

The centerpiece of the kitchen is the mahogany refrigerator cabinet. It's part armoire, part breakfront, part china cabinet. We installed mercury glass in lieu of transparent panes to reflect what is happening in the rest of the kitchen. On the beds, antique chenille spreads play off pillows sporting hyper-enlarged Colonial prints. Both feature old-fashioned forms used in a modern way, a theme that carries throughout the house.

The foyer, right, features a harlequin checkerboard marble floor. A mahogany Charles X table with a marble top from France, circa 1830, is the space's centerpiece. PREVIOUS PAGE AND ABOVE: A picket fence marks the entrance to this white clapboard Key West beach house, which was renovated with an eye to making it brighter and slightly more formal.

A richly toned wooden vanity from Waterworks, left, sits against a gray marble wall. Above, hibiscus and a palm seed stalk add a tropical note. PREVIOUS PAGES, LEFT: In the kitchen, cabinetry intended to emulate a breakfront china cabinet houses the refrigerator and pantry. PREVIOUS PAGES, RIGHT: The staircase in the front hall curves elegantly as it ascends to the second floor.

A Murano glass fish, above, sits on a glass-topped table. Hatteras wood rockers, right, are painted with an aqua wash. PREVIOUS PAGES: In the living room, Anthony Ardavin's abstract painting *Awakening Sun* hangs over the sofa. The metal chairs with polished frames are vintage John Salterini. Chinese figurines stand on a black split-bamboo cocktail table, which in turn rests on a Stark carpet that melds elements of a fisherman-knit sweater with an Asian motif.

Matte white paint helps a taxidermy sailfish, above, to become a focal point on a wall covered in chocolate-colored grass cloth. The sconces were sourced at Urban Electric. Embroidered vintage cotton depicting sea life helps a modern chair, left, live happily in a room featuring traditional architectural details.

Comfortable seating and lanterns, above, beckon visitors to admire the view into the sunset.
A corner of the master bedroom, right, features a vintage Cuban screen of woven banana leaves.
The diamond-weave carpet is made from the leaf fibers of abaca. The lime-green pillow is covered in Mongolian lamb's wool. PREVIOUS PAGES: Walls covered in a gray silk bring a little shimmer
into the master bedroom—a theme completed by a lacquered William Switzer bamboo four-poster
bed and brass-clad side tables with nail-head detailing. The bedspread is vintage chenille.

Mahogany beds, left, found at the Brimfield Antique Show in Massachusetts provide a strong note in a boy's bedroom. Vintage semaphore flags found in their original packages were framed individually. A girl's bedroom, above, features a pine antique secretary and a Blacksmith Blossom Chair by Serge Rosenzweig. The bedspread is vintage chenille. PREVIOUS PAGES: The master bathroom, which picks up on the suite's overall color scheme, features fixtures from Waterworks.

classical

We treasure those rare opportunities to design a project from start to finish, and here we had the pleasure of selecting everything from the front door right down to the napkin rings on the table. This house is known as Seraphim Point, and it occupies a very enviable site within the Ocean Reef Club in Key Largo, the northernmost of the Florida Keys. Its location on a private peninsula allowed us to situate the house with all its major views to the west, over the water, and thus to Florida's majestic sunsets.

The clients' permanent home is in Cincinnati; when we visited, it was clear that their taste inclined toward all things British, so together we decided to design this house in the Anglo-Caribbean—also sometimes called the Caribbean Regency—style. We love it because it's at once formal and tropical. We leavened the more serious, classical aspects of the architecture with whimsical nautical overtones. Our stylized approach was to take something formal and make it more tropical by making it more relaxed.

From the start, it was clear that this was a magical site. An entry lined by two rows of banyan trees creates a green canopy overhead as visitors arrive. We were privileged to work with the Palm Beach landscape architecture firm of Sanchez and Maddux, who also created a wraparound bayfront lawn and an elegant bowl-shaped swimming pool.

The house itself rests on a base of native Florida keystone. Windows feature traditional Caribbean shutters, the roof is wood shake, and there is elaborate stucco detailing on the walls. Inside and out the balconies and stairways have wrought-iron railings taken from what is probably a seventeenth-century French design that we used to soften the house, to give it more plasticity—it has its share of edges and angles.

The foyer adds to the sense of wonder. The walls are hewn from solid pieces of Florida keystone, a native oolitic limestone filled with fossilized shells and other mementos of the sea. Everything in the house comes from a neoclassical vocabulary. The foyer floor, for example, is the traditional circle and square; it's all matte buffed rather than highly polished stone. Its pattern was inspired by the loggia of Miami's great historic house museum, Vizcaya.

This is a two-story house with five bedrooms, but it is also oriented toward outdoor living, and there is a focus on carrying details that appear outside through to the inside. Bracketed ceilings, for example, have the same detail as the keystone. For ceilings that feature exposed wood, we chose types reminiscent of driftwood; the library is also paneled in highly textured, local pecky cypress.

The entire interior color scheme's inspiration and palette derives from the first objects bought for the house—a pair of cloisonné lamps of celadon, citron, pink, and blue. Inspiration from other objects and contexts abounds, too: the "china room" was designed around an oversized export bowl and the dining chairs were hand-painted with dragonflies, bees, and other "famous" Florida pests.

Special touches appear everywhere. The guest lounge features hand-painted nautical charts. The kitchen/breakfast room/wine-tasting area was inspired by a comparable room in the owners' Ohio home, but the breakfast area is set apart by a set of curved, bifold doors made in Germany that allow the room to open out onto the pool terrace. The master bedroom has a vaulted ceiling and expansive windows; it is also sited closest to the water and, in many ways, offers the feeling of being on a yacht.

At night the sunset reflects onto the bay and, in turn, its colors infuse the house with color. At that time of day, its presence is almost majestic, reflecting the reflection of the reflection.

Reiterating the decorative pattern used on the exterior, a nickel-topped handrail, above, curves along the main stair. A carved mahogany fish and antique brass crayfish, right, sit on a hall table underneath a wood-and-silver-leaf chandelier. PREVIOUS PAGES: The entry hall features an antique Swedish table with bronze "lion paw" feet. Its floor includes three different, honed marbles, and its walls are carved keystone panels.

Opening directly onto an outdoor room, the living room requires furniture and upholstery that can stand up to the elements—in this case Sutherland furniture with Perennials upholstery. The vintage gold-leafed bamboo chair was found at Mecox Gardens in Palm Beach, and the cocktail table is a vintage Baker piece. The living room carpet is a Delft-blue linen.

To play on the deep colors found in the Florida Keys, the pool, above, is designed in an "extreme blue" hue. The outdoor fireplace, right, is also tropical in inspiration—hand-carved Florida keystone—and vintage shell-motif andirons are painted white to continue the neutral theme.

Famille rose antique lamps with five facets, each in a different color, inspired this living room's color scheme. It also features an "almost-matched" pair of Belgian chests in stripped, bleached oak. Indigo-hued, coarse grass cloth walls and a painting entitled *Cockatoo Footwash*, by Hunt Slonem, help the dining room relate to adjoining spaces. The yellow, lacquered ceramic vegetables are by Robert Kuo.

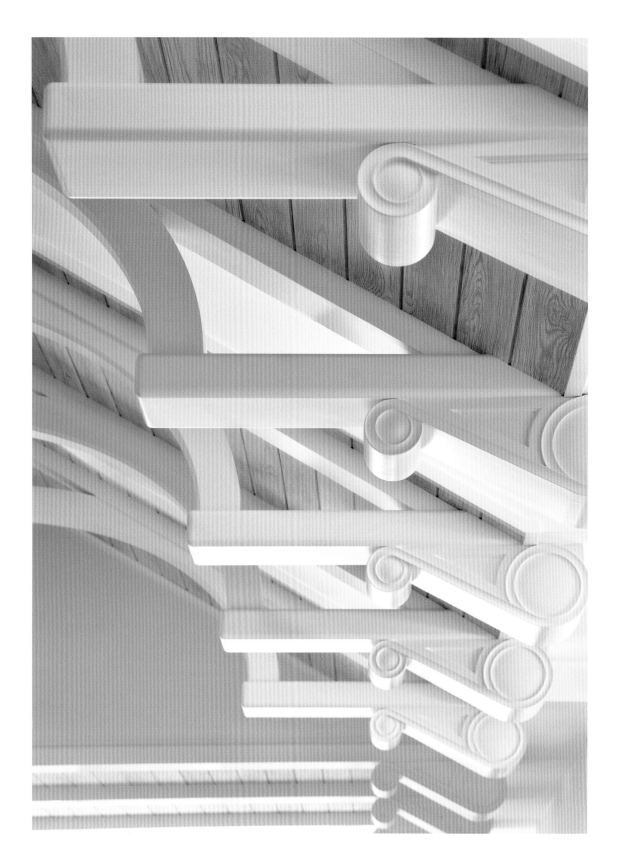

Decorative wooden brackets support the eaves, above. In the morning room, right, the seating is covered in a hand-woven palm rope chain by John Himmel that re-creates a French 1940s design. The circular flatweave carpet features tangerine and white stripes. PREVIOUS PAGES: The backsplash in the kitchen is blue celestial marble, which appropriately conjures images of the vibrant Florida sky. The limed oak cabinetry incorporates Swedish diamond details, and the floor is composed of randomly flagged, broken limestone.

Barley-twist stools with rush seats, left, pull up to a wine tasting area with a whimsical antique bottle dispenser in a corner of the kitchen. *It's a Reef Cup Kind of Day*, a painting by Guy Harvey, was commissioned by the owner to commemorate a memorable day's catch. It hangs near a nautically themed, custom bar made of marine-varnished mahogany in the game room.

In this bedroom, the carpet is woven abaca, while the walls have a Madagascar covering. The indoor bed is bamboo, while the outdoor bed on the terrace is made of teak and is covered with a Perennials fabric. The tambour table is carved marble with a flower motif.

Reflective surfaces define this bathroom, left and above. A white lacquer "grotto chair" paired with a vintage desk transforms the match into a vanity; its lamp bases are made from celadon jade carved into birds. The mirrors over the sinks have shell and fish motifs. A neoclassical starburst pattern in three colors of marble reinforces the room's geometry. The chandelier, which was once the main fixture in a Florida department store, is vintage Dorothy Draper.

Coral-colored grass cloth on the walls of this bedroom complements the intense ocean blue seen through its windows, above. The four-poster bed, right, is mahogany and features notched headboard panels. A collection of plaster intaglio set into an antique window frame hangs above. Wool-and-silk rugs in a lattice pattern sit on bleached, hand-scraped oak floors.

Nautical charts of local waters hand-painted by artist Joel Blanco cover one wall of this office. The maritime theme is carried further by the use of snap-ties on the roller shades, mahogany stools with nickel foot rails, and a brass steam gauge. OVERLEAF: The bunk room carries on the theme. Beds feature railings with sea horse carvings and shell-printed curtains, while decorative accents like starfish throw pillows on Adirondack chairs and a blue-and-white striped rug complete the look.

memorable

This house holds enormous importance for us, and though it is now two decades old we still cherish it—and are proud of it. The owners, Rance Crain and his late wife Merrilee, were among our first clients, and it was by their grace that we truly began to develop our "classic coastal" style. This mature home proves that architecture in Florida is not necessarily only of the moment, not inevitably trendy.

The Crains honeymooned in Bermuda and fell in love with the particular British Colonial style so emblematic of that island country. Thus, the house features a scalloped parapet over the main entrance and such details as dentils and oval windows. The interiors reflect formal English style, but lightened and brightened. It serves as a family of five's primary residence and so needs a measure of livability.

The walls and details are all made of textured stucco. A true Bermuda house would have had a white roof, but that was prohibited in the Windermere community where the home is situated.

The house is on the shore of one of the numerous inland lakes that dot Central Florida near Orlando—Lake Butler—and the nightly fireworks display at Walt Disney World is visible, at a distance, from the patio. Its

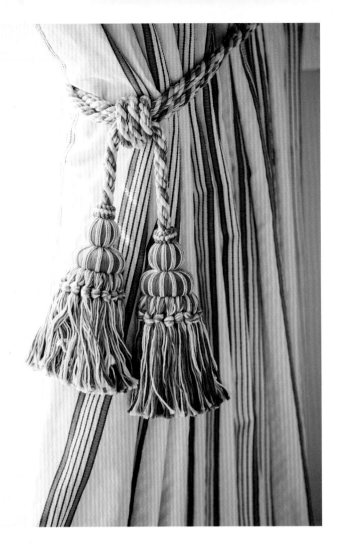

pool is set at the water's edge, and alligators often hide under the dock.

When we first took the job, Merrilee Crain gave us a detailed list of everything the house needed to include, with square footages already figured out—right down to how much space was required for pet food storage. To this day, we've never seen anything else so precise. The family loves dogs and collects books, so the house needed to accommodate both passions. A final plan that encompassed 14,000 square feet, three floors, and twenty-three rooms met its needs.

The house features extensive millwork that conveys a traditional mood. The color scheme rests on pale greens that reflect the cypress trees romantically draped with Spanish moss in the landscape. Much of the furniture was inherited, as were a number of the chandeliers in the house; this provided Phyllis an opportunity to increase her knowledge of certain antiques, in particular how to work with and appreciate them in a contemporary interior.

When we went back to see the house not long ago, we were highly moved to find that almost nothing had been changed. Its classic architecture and interiors ensure that it will continue to stand the test of time.

PREVIOUS PAGE AND OPPOSITE: Walnut herringbone floors inlaid with hand-painted marquetry in the front hall introduce custom craftsmanship that continues throughout the house. A replica of *Nike of Samothrace*, also known as *Winged Victory*, stands on the newel post. Signed drawings by Henri de Toulouse-Lautrec hang on the wall.

A landscaped pathway of broken keystone pavers, above, leads to an herb garden. An arcade, right, connects the breakfast room and the guest cottage. Its floor is made of Saturnia stone, and the benches are antique wrought iron. PREVIOUS PAGES: The owners honeymooned in Bermuda and decided on a Bermuda-style house for their permanent residence.

Baccarat hurricane lamps, above, flank a silver tray that holds crystal decanters. A vintage Sergio Bustamante copper-and-brass parrot, right, perches above celadon green Asian garden seats with raised floral decorations. The curtains are dupioni silk. PREVIOUS PAGES: A fine collection of antique seating rests on one of the house's many custom-made rugs.

Animal-print fabrics, above, begin a faunal theme that extends to a Castillo silver carafe from Mexico with a parrot-shaped handle made of turquoise, top right, and a teak wooden bench with a jaguar carved at one end, lower left. Cast aluminum chairs, opposite, circle a stone-topped table. PREVIOUS PAGES: A porch room offers an exquisite and intimate connection between inside and out via large windows and views to Lake Butler.

An oculus window draws the eye up to the master suite's high ceilings while double doors open onto the subtropical landscape. A four-poster bed features palm-topped finials that match the deep tones of a French marble-topped table and French caned chairs. The leaf-patterned custom carpet is hand-tufted.

Pools by Maurice Fatio from the Palm Beach of the 1920s and 1930s inspired this oval incarnation. OPPOSITE, CLOCKWISE FROM TOP LEFT: A gate leading to an orange grove, the pool at twilight, Lake Butler, and a waterfall that cascades into the pool.

environmental

When Donna Shalala became president of the University of Miami in 2001, she at first settled into the existing president's house—a tropical colonial residence in Coral Gables. The university, however, had been bequeathed Smathers Four Fillies Farm in 1993, which happened to be one of the city's largest undeveloped tracts of land. Shalala determined to build a new home there that would suit not just her immediate needs, but the university's and its future presidents' needs as well.

The firm of Duany Plater-Zyberk and Company—and more specifically Elizabeth Plater-Zyberk, who was at the time the long-standing dean of the university's school of architecture—was selected to design what would come to be known as Ibis House, after the university's tropical bird mascot. The structure needed to feel at once intimate and welcoming; hundreds of people were to be entertained there each week. Its mood therefore had to be both ceremonial and livable.

The site, in a native hammock of abundant old oaks and exotic tropical plant specimens, provided the opportunity to introduce tropical elements. A U-shaped plan was developed with two wings that splay to create an open courtyard and house eighteen rooms. Arriving guests step first into a curved foyer that opens directly onto the courtyard, then move through a music room, the living room, and eventually reach the dining room. Its tables can be separated into smaller, conversation-inducing arrangements or pulled together, banquet style. At the end of an evening meal, coffee and dessert are served at a large round table that is the centerpiece of the foyer.

Ibis House is a LEED-certified building, so we determined that the interiors would follow suit. Its materials are derived, as much as possible, from local sources or made from recycled materials in order to narrow its carbon footprint. To convey a tropical feel we used grass cloth, a renewable material, on the walls. The "boce" lights in the stairwells are made of recycled glass, and the dining room chandeliers and kitchen backsplashes are made from recycled aluminum cans.

The black, taupe, and light-gray tiles found throughout the house on almost every surface where tile could go have a shimmering quality derived from inset seashells and sand and make a strong statement, almost like terrazzo. They are created by a local craftswoman; for this project, they were enhanced with iridescent Atlantic beach shells. We used them in a variety of patterns, from checkerboard to stripes to diamonds, throughout the house, on borders, insets, and reliefs. The unadorned architecture required a bold interior statement so the floors became a focal point, softened by custom area rugs and drapes. Plater-Zyberk admires the work of Edwin Lutyens, an English architect active in the late nineteenth and early twentieth centuries, so we turned to his work for inspiration on many of these patterns, and for the custom-made rugs. Even the living room ceiling refers to his work—it is Lutyens-esque academic in style.

The palette moves from subtle and muted to daringly bright. We drew the living room color scheme of green and silver from the hues of the old oaks that sit on the land, yet elsewhere the colors are more vibrant to reflect both President Shalala's personality and the youth of the students. Several of the carpets feature palm frond motifs that again reflect the setting. Much of the furniture had been custom-made for the president's previous house, so here it was reupholstered, for example with a Rose Cumming historic print in indoor-outdoor fabric for the kitchen.

Bands of cream and gray stone tiles from SeaStone flooring accentuate the length of the gallery while striped linen drapes bordered with a Greek key pattern draw attention to its height. An arrangement of ceramic plates by Picasso is clustered on the far wall to create a focal point. PREVIOUS PAGE: A contemporary interpretation of a porte-cochère greets visitors to Ibis House, which was designed by Elizabeth Plater-Zyberk, dean of the University of Miami School of Architecture until mid-2013.

Scroll-like forms appear in a wrought-iron stair railing, a cross-section of a conch shell embedded in a floor tile, and the Greek key trim of long drapes, above. The stairwell lighting is made of orbs of recycled green, white, and clear glass. Traditional white wainscoting lines a stairwell, right, while a coral-banded wool runner injects a tropical note. PREVIOUS PAGES: Diamond shapes in the flooring create a natural frame for a hall table.

Environmentally friendly
materials and pieces reign in
the dining room, such as
modern chandeliers shaped
like tree branches fabricated
from recycled aluminum cans
by Christopher Poehlmann
of CP Lighting, wall covering
made from recycled paper,
and a simple indoor-outdoor
sisal rug. Dining tables can
be arranged separately
for a homey look or moved
together to accommodate
large, formal functions.

A mantel carved from local Florida keystone, above, features a transitional form. The painting above is by Guillermo Wiederman. Palm fronds rendered in wool and silk inject a hint of the tropics in a rug custom designed by Stephanie Odegard, left. Ceiling fans all run on one motor, an environmental gesture. The double-tiered chandelier is by David Iatesta.

Lanterns, above and opposite, are from Urban Electric. The work of the British architect Edwin Lutyens was a source of inspiration for both the plasterwork on the ceiling and the choice of furniture in a sitting room. The rug was designed by Stephanie Odegard, and the antique Indian table is made of rosewood that pairs well with the room's other dark-wood notes. A glass sculpture by Therman Statom rests on top.

An overscaled chevron pattern on the rug is a vibrant foil to walls demurely covered in smoky, charcoal gray grass cloth. Twin daybeds are placed back-to-back to function as sectional seating. PREVIOUS PAGES: The kitchen features tri-colored SeaStone flooring tile arranged in a checkerboard pattern. Walls of grasshopper-green grass cloth accentuate the bold colors of a durable, indoor-outdoor Rose Cumming reissue fabric on the banquette. Chamcha-wood tables from Indonesia and a kitchen island topped with bamboo continue the house's tropical theme.

Spanish moss, above, hangs delicately from ancient oaks surrounding the house. Linen drapes with embroidered palm leaves, right, bring some vegetation indoors. Modern lanterns along the ceiling by Vaughan Lighting reinforce the rhythm of the windows and the banding on the floor.

Good design from different eras unites; an heirloom desk, above, from Donna Shalala's family sits under a large-scale sunburst mirror by Albert Hadley. Three colors of SeaStone are used to make a plaid-patterned floor in a bathroom, right. The walls feature wainscoting of fossil stone with imprinted shells and a seafoam-green grass cloth.

personal

More often than not we work on projects sited on limited lots, so this house, which sits on an acre and a half next to a lake, was a real opportunity. Even better, there was some terrain—for Florida. The land is elevated by ten feet and both inclines and steps down.

The owners of this house, Susan and Larry Kahn, wanted a quintessential Florida living space—a covered outdoor room. They were realists, though, so it had to be screened to provide protection from sun and bugs. This full-blown, outdoor living room often called a "Florida Room" became the central feature of the house.

We have long been inspired not just by Mediterranean-style architecture in Florida, but even more by the refined, Spanish-inspired designs of George Washington Smith and Wallace Neff found in California. For this home we drew on our visits there and on our personal research as well. The structure is clothed in tradition, but it flows like a modern house.

This is a large house—10,000 square feet and sixteen rooms. The tile roofs are genuine, hand-made barrel tile. Details such as brackets, columns, and balustrades all add to the sense of architectural authenticity. The ornamental wrought iron on the exterior is repeated on the inside, along stairways especially.

A formal two-story living room with a minstrels' gallery and porthole windows provides a second area for entertaining. It was inspired by a 40-foot-long living room the owner's grandfather had built in a house in

Arkansas in the 1920s. Its coral rock fireplace was inspired by a similar mantel in the Al Capone Suite at the Coral Gables Biltmore Hotel.

The rugs were collected by Phyllis during her travels to play off the house's floors of light and dark Jerusalem gold limestone and hand-hewn walnut. One of the most important rugs that now graces the dining room was found at a Saturday market in Woodstock, New York. The tangerine and avocado green used throughout the house are intended to be reminiscent of the fruit groves located nearby. The walls are stucco both inside and out, but the interior walls are custom-textured to suggest age without imparting a feeling of heaviness and were kept in a fresh white to brighten the rooms that are enlivened by these bright citrus hues.

Collections of works by the Everglades painter A. E. "Beanie" Backus hang in the living room and foyer, along with an inherited set of Thomas Hart Benton works on paper that hung in Larry Kahn's bedroom when he was a young boy. Most of the furniture comes from the owners' previous houses, but reupholstering it helped it fit well in this new abode.

Gold and cream Jerusalem stone create a checkerboard pattern in the foyer. The furniture includes a pedestal table by Ebanista and a deacon's bench from Century Furniture. PREVIOUS PAGES: Elegant elements from Spanish Colonial Revival houses in Southern California translate well to this home in Coral Gables, where the dominant architectural style is Mediterranean.

Shaped by the architectural footprint of the house, a terrace, above, holds a stone table from the clients' previous home. The dining room, right, carries on the citrus theme prevalent throughout the house. Lime and lemon hues found in an oriental rug from the Jalils Rug Collection, green Phillip Jeffries grass cloth walls, and side and arm chairs covered in Highland Court cotton-and-wool crewel are complemented by wide-plank black walnut flooring. PREVIOUS PAGES: The living room adopts citrus orange for warmth, iterated in striped chairs from Century, an antique oriental rug, and floral-upholstered armchairs—Taylor & Taylor finds. The carved Florida keystone fireplace is flanked by plaster reliefs that frame the entrance to a walnut-paneled library.

116

In the kitchen, an iron chandelier hangs from a brick barrel ceiling while an oversized lantern hangs over a pedestal table. The custom round banquette in the breakfast nook is covered in a bright tropical fabric, while the white lacquer chairs are covered in moss-colored vinyl. OVERLEAF: A pecky cypress ceiling adds an undeniably tropical feel to a screened-in, outdoor living room. Curved sofas with an abundance of soft pillows encourage lingering and conversation, and dining chairs of hand-glazed, weatherproof aluminum faux bamboo offer a place for meals alfresco.

monumental

We love history, we love to travel, and we love to visit important historic houses—always sources of great inspiration. In this expansive, 140-acre waterfront compound on Lake Thonotosassa, to the northeast of Tampa, we paid homage to some of the most memorable we have seen: Biltmore House in Asheville, North Carolina; The Breakers in Newport, Rhode Island; and Versailles.

The site where this house and its ancillary buildings are located was once covered in orange groves that ended in a fringe of cypress trees at the lakeshore, but today it embraces gardens, trails, wooded drives, pastures, and even a go-cart track. The house itself was designed in the French Norman style by the Tampa-based architectural firm of Cooper Johnson Smith; we were selected to provide the interior architecture and interior design, as well as the outdoor furniture.

We sought to capitalize on the architecture by creating interiors that were predominantly in the French country style, but with an understated splendor and, of course, allusions to the past. The French have held a fascination with Florida for centuries, and their similar enthusiasm for oranges—which first came to Europe from China—made the adoption of a citrus theme a natural choice. At an antique fabric fair in London, we also happened across a tiny, 200-year-old fragment of fabric from the Palace of Fontainebleau that corresponds to the time Napoleon lived there. It became the inspiration for the colors seen in the long living room—we loved it because it married our two main sources of inspiration. The living room measures 30 by 100 feet, so the Hall of Mirrors at Versailles also came to mind as a source of inspiration—we installed paned mirrors along the length of one wall to reflect the view from outside. The library is paneled in a hand-carved walnut similar to a treatment we saw at The Breakers, and the loggia at another Vanderbilt family

mansion, Biltmore House, offered us ideas for the family "hearth room."

We've always loved the way America's Gilded Age houses unabashedly display faux finishes that simulate marble, stone, or wood alongside truly luxurious materials. In this house, the foyer features hand-painted faux stone vaulting; the dining room walls are covered in custom, hand-painted silk wallpaper depicting orange trees inspired by the site and also Florida palms in a tropical adaptation of the classic bamboo-and-plum-blossom design; and, like the great houses of eras past, the kitchen is fitted with marble countertops and backsplashes. It also looks out to a large and productive *jardin potager*.

Clients with widespread interests and enthusiasms, most particularly for sports and the sporting life, make this house unique in many ways. The complex includes a two-story guest cottage, horse stables, barns, a dovecote, and garages for twelve family vehicles along with some twenty-eight collectors' cars, four limousines, four recreational vehicles, and numerous go-carts and even motor-powered bicycles. The owners are racing aficionados but they also love fashion so we tried to give the house the sensibility of an estate owned by a French *bon vivant* from the early part of the twentieth century.

A view over Lake Thonotosassa, above. An antique Italian walnut secretary, opposite, is home to a collection of white-and-gold porcelain lattice compotes, as well as a collection of ceramic swans and vases from the 1930s. A French Directoire ebony daybed rests on a citron carpet featuring a pattern of flowers and vines. PREVIOUS PAGE: A French wrought-iron Art Deco foyer table was retrofitted with a French limestone top that holds Murano-glass flamingoes. Limestone in gray and cream hues is honed and pillowed to form a checkerboard-pattern floor.

Details from the Long Room, clockwise from top left, include a vintage crystal-and-black-glass table that holds a French candy dish, pillows with floral silk fragments from the Palace of Fontainebleau, stylized Louis XVI chairs, and Moroccan-inspired drapery. A vintage brass birdcage, opposite, rests on a long table. PREVIOUS PAGES: The Hall of Mirrors at Versailles inspired this space. The walls are covered with Swedish milk paint in a gray-green hue with gold leaf detail while the floors are covered in custom carpets featuring a pattern of black-and-white flowers on an acid-green field.

Dining room walls, right, come to life thanks to a silk mural depicting oranges and palms. The Italian bench in the background features finely detailed carvings covered in gold leaf and upholstery of broad panels of tangerine and white silk. The French chandeliers sparkle thanks to triple rock crystal. Two blanc de chine figurative cascading compotes hold citrus fruits and stand on a walnut extension table. Antique French country chairs purchased at Cedric DuPont Antiques are upholstered in checkered silk to complete the space.

Even the most functional of rooms receive attention to detail. Mud room walls, above, are made of broken, random-pattern stone and a humble potting table is elevated with a zinc top and brass nail heads. The kitchen, opposite, includes a chateau-patterned limestone floor and a blue-veined quartzite backsplash. The pot rack over the center island is from Ann Morris. PREVIOUS PAGES: Louis XVIII *bergères* with embroidered backs are a focal point in the parlor. Other pieces include a linen rug, a pair of French Bombay chests with marble tops, and a 1950s glass-and-brass coffee table.

The Men's Lounge, above and opposite, offers guests ample and comfortable seating
with an inglenook bench dotted with cushions covered in Clarence House fabric and
a semicircular sectional sofa with a faux-alligator back and linen herringbone upholstery.
A Moroccan table with metal appliqué and leather tassels found in Morocco and
a tapestry purchased by the clients in France enhance the room's Old-World mood.

Green cotton velvet covers club chairs, left, that flank an antique Moroccan trunk embellished with malachite inlay and appliqué. A jute carpet by Doris Leslie Blau sits on a wood floor made of scrubbed oak and draws the eye into an adjacent Pub Room that boasts a mood-setting chandelier of alabaster.

The fireplace in the Hearth Room, above, is of Texas limestone. Window treatments depicting monochromatic sunflowers hang over two sets of French doors. The cocktail table is made of reclaimed wood and is by Dos Gallos. A walnut pedestal table, opposite, is unexpectedly paired with reed-backed Orkney chairs. The room's hand-braided rug was custom crafted in Pennsylvania. Majolica plates featuring citrus fruits tie the room to the rest of the house's theme.

A bedroom, above, features antique "raspberry knot" linens that Phyllis Taylor found at the Portobello Road Market in London. A bathroom floor, left, becomes a decorative item of note thanks to a combination of Cuban tile and terrazzo from Waterworks. The marble-topped sinks have antiqued, oil-rubbed, bronze-finished fixtures, also from Waterworks. Latticework cabinet doors conceal storage.

Black-and-white-striped
awnings and cushions in
Sunbrella fabric bring a taste
of the Côte d'Azur to
an outdoor seating area.
Resin Adirondack chairs in a
lilac hue add a contemporary
note to the ensemble.

historical

Our clients on this project wanted an "inheritable" family home, one that dug its roots deep into its location—in this case the mouth of the Tarpon River where it flows into the New River in Fort Lauderdale—and into history as well. A style with English antecedents appealed to them, so together we came to Tudor. This home is related to the sprawling American Tudor houses found in early-twentieth-century suburbs, but adapted for the Florida climate. The challenge here was to make a nontropical house that fit in a tropical setting. To accomplish that, we kept the woodwork light and gave it deep, outsized windows. We also wrapped a veranda around three sides of the house and ensured that the circulation plan would make indoor-outdoor living a true possibility. The house is basically composed of two wings that seem at once inviting and protective. This architectural move broadens the views available from inside and also gives the house a sense of generosity when viewed from the outside.

In essence, this is a grand cottage with rough stucco, rusticated limestone quoins, leaded windows, and a slate roof inspired by English architect Edwin Lutyens. Details that evoke England abound in the architecture and the interior finishes. There are nineteen rooms in all, including a Moorish-influenced, walnut-paneled library and an Old English–style pub with stained glass. Throughout the house there are bay windows and four-centered limestone arches as well as checkerboard marble floors, bleached oak paneling, and carved balustrades. The kitchen island was derived from a Lutyens design, there is quatrefoil tile in the master bath, and the powder room doors are carved with Gothic arches.

To instill a sense of age, we searched for pieces of furniture that didn't originate in Florida but that—whether by fate or fortune—ended up here. The library desk, for example, is nineteenth-century Biedermeier with inlaid mother-of-pearl panels. When items that were exactly right eluded us, we designed them. A carpet for the family room was inspired by an antique floral-print textile we'd seen; we exploded the design and commissioned a custom rug from it—at one point, when we worried that it was taking too long, we contacted the people in Thailand who were working on it, but they sent us a photo of two women weaving it on a loom and we were so moved by that image of their hands and faces that we decided it was definitely worth the wait.

We have always embraced the idea that every space—even a transitional space—counts. Accordingly, we try to make every square foot of a house interesting. You may not have formal dinners every night, perhaps, but you inevitably traverse rooms that are not heavily used; thus it's worth adding features like family foyers or inglenooks, charming spaces that make you want to spend time in them and that help you live in the whole house.

The front entrance, above, reveals gables clad in limestone and a decidedly English sensibility. In the husband's Pub Room, right, antiqued oak is punctuated with stained glass and paired with an Edwardian leather club chair. PREVIOUS PAGE: Limed oak panels along the stair were designed to evoke the work of Edwin Lutyens. Floors of gray and white Paris ceramic tiles in a checkerboard pattern add a sense of age. OVERLEAF: The Tudor-style arch on the carved stone fireplace is one of many found throughout the house. An opulently patterned wool-and-silk rug from Stark Carpet and a French nineteenth-century chandelier add Old-World touches that transport visitors far from tropical Florida.

Black and white fabrics—including rosette embroidery on a canopy chair—play off the vibrant red hue of stitched wallpaper from Maya Romanoff in a dining room. A sunburst-top dining table from Dessin Fournir, a limed-oak console from John Hutton, and a weathered mahogany, crystal, and steel chandelier from David Iatesta add dimension to the space. PREVIOUS PAGES, LEFT: A set of French Moroccan colored lanterns from the 1920s is placed in front of a window to reflect the light. PREVIOUS PAGES, RIGHT: Three tiers of a Fortuny chandelier light a study that also features a Gustavian Swedish daybed and a large Austrian desk of Thuya wood veneer from circa 1910.

Ceiling beams made from reclaimed wood evoke the great halls of historic houses and call for accessories of equally imposing scale. An oversized custom lantern by Urban Electric fills the space above a large seating area, and an area rug below by Patterson, Flynn & Martin was custom-designed with an overscaled floral pattern. The Louis XVI–style bibliothèques along the far wall are nine-teenth-century French.

Accessories that feature or relate to *le coq*, above, add a French country note to the house. Wood panels glazed in a grayish-green hue, a banister sporting a quatrefoil design, and a reclaimed brick floor add coziness to a family foyer, right. PREVIOUS PAGES: Vintage, stylized high-back chairs painted a candy-apple red are pulled up to a custom marble-topped kitchen table. Like other rooms in the house, the kitchen features paneled walls of limed oak.

The bedroom, left and above, is papered in a vegetal design from
Schumacher while wood furnishings continue the motif. A four-poster bed
fits snugly into a Tudor niche in the wall and a desk and chair from William
Switzer offer a place for perusing a book or the day's correspondence.

Gray marble cut with a waterjet into a quatrefoil pattern by Waterworks lines a bathroom's walls and floor. Suitably glamorous accessories for the space include a Venetian glass mirror and a vintage Art Deco vanity. A chandelier from Ironies casts a warm glow over a freestanding bathtub, echoed by light from rock crystal wall sconces from Charles Edward.

Wrought-iron poolside
seating from Formations
Outdoor Furniture and a
canopy chair from Century
beckon visitors to wile away
the daylight hours; even in
the evenings, however, a
lantern from Urban Electric
allows the covered outdoor
space to be appreciated.

Historic elements from the main house's interior carry over into the pool house as well. The oversize chandelier is antiqued pewter, and a Welsh dresser made of English oak, circa 1830, holds a collection of brightly colored dinnerware. The swiveling bar stools are from Quintus. Gallery rails above the refrigerators hold a collection of salt and pepper shakers. OVERLEAF: The architecture of the house is Tudor in origin, but the deep blue sky is definitively Floridian.

perennial

This winter home at the Ocean Reef Club in Key Largo reflects our architecture and interior finishes. While it draws on Florida's great and imaginative tradition of Spanish design, it does so with a light hand and a tropical touch. The site, at the end of a cul-de-sac where two canals meet, gives extra meaning to the idea of a "waterfront location."

The house's single story wraps around an entry courtyard. By positioning the front entrance along the street's curve, we were able to give this four-bedroom house the kind of winsome street presence that historic homes so often have. A two-car garage—plus extra space for golf carts—is tucked around to the side. In back, an elevated pool, deck, and a two-story gazebo look out over the confluence of the two canals.

To give the house an even more authentic feel, we used hand-finished stucco on both the exterior and interior walls—which also helps to keep the house cool—and inserted hand-forged wrought iron detailing. The roof is likewise covered in hand-made barrel tile. Warm-toned Saltillo tiles, so typical of Spanish-style architecture, extend the use of solid, traditional materials deep into the interior.

We drew on numerous sources for the design of this house, including Mexican precedents. We wanted it to have the type of romance associated with old, remote, even ancient and crumbling structures. The wrought-iron balustrades on the house feature decorative planter brackets, an architectural detail we first encountered in our own office in an

adapted Miami Beach bungalow. Similarly, the staircase was designed to be reminiscent of the haciendas of San Miguel de Allende.

Like many contemporary houses, a single "great room" contains the living and dining rooms and flows into the kitchen. At one end, we designed a unique, hacienda-inspired fireplace. To provide balance at the other end, a prominent archway leads into the kitchen.

To allow easy flow between inside and out, the house makes extensive use of loggias and French doors. We also took the opportunity to create a mirador topped by a decorative parapet on the roof deck to provide further unexpected outdoor space. To customize the plan while taking the owner's particular needs into consideration, we honored his wish for a private office by separating it from the main house; its exterior wall, however, was arranged so that it defines the perimeter of the courtyard. Greiwe Interiors worked with the owner to customize the furnishings.

In many ways, this house typifies our architectural practice. We embrace history and love and respect classical and traditional architectural styles, but our houses are very much designed for today's families. We embrace both the technology we now have at our fingertips and the lifestyles of our post-millennial times.

A curtained seating area, above, provides shaded outdoor space. A simply coffered interior loggia connects the house's kitchen and service wing to its bedroom wing. Both the Saltillo tile on the floor and the textured stucco hint at Mexican influences on the design. Moorish rugs and prayer stools were furnished by Greiwe Interiors. PREVIOUS PAGE: Wrought-iron details including an ornate entry gate and a candlelit chandelier reference this Mexican-inspired home's historical precedents.

A simple, sculptural fireplace, opposite, is the focal point of the large central living room, which is casually furnished in white slipcovered furniture. The art, furniture, and decorative objects, like those above, were selected to reflect a sympathetic, handcrafted elegance.

ABOVE, CLOCKWISE FROM TOP LEFT: The courtyard features an antique fountain and a staircase with risers tiled in alternating colors that leads to a mirador overlooking Florida Bay. The house has architectural details intended to be discovered gradually, such as wrought-iron planter brackets. The design of the tiled, domed gazebo was inspired by a well that William Taylor saw in Oaxaca. An arched entryway fitted with wrought-iron gates in an open pattern, opposite, allows a welcoming glimpse into the courtyard beyond.

179

tropical

This Fisher Island house benefits from a true one-of-a-kind setting. Its views extend across an exquisitely landscaped golf course to Miami's Government Cut ship channel, with both the Atlantic Ocean and the southern tip of Miami Beach visible beyond. For almost two decades, the island was the private winter playground of William Kissam Vanderbilt II, who docked his 264-foot yacht there and built himself a villa in a refined Mediterranean style. When the still-exclusive, 100-acre island was eventually developed as a winter resort, only twenty-eight single-family residences were constructed, and the architectural style set by Vanderbilt was retained.

We collaborated on the interior architecture and interior design of this rather grand, fifteen-room house. Our goal was to turn the existing structure into a true home, one that luxuriates in the crisp, compelling, bright colors of the tropics. We were able to work within the architectural envelope to open the house up to the brilliance of Florida's sunlight and its cooling ocean breezes. The house's circulation revolves around a courtyard, but it also features covered terraces and loggias that connect this house to its beautiful surroundings.

Conceptually, this project was like a townhouse with a central courtyard that introduces light into the center of the structure. Typically, in Florida, waterfront property is so precious that lots are carved up into narrow slivers, so architects here often only focus on designing a house's front and a back; they are seldom concerned about what happens in between. The courtyard was really created as a light well to illuminate what would otherwise be a long, dark interior with plenty of Florida sunlight.

The design draws on numerous classical elements while maintaining its connection to time and place. A traditional curving staircase features a decorative wrought-iron rail with a modern motif, for example, which rises up through the two-story, oval foyer. To keep a visual rhythm, that same wrought-iron design echoes the motif on the entry door.

The interior design needed to convey subtlety and sophistication befitting the house and its enviable setting, but we also wanted it to celebrate the joy of island life. We opted for a palette in exotic citrus colors that symbolize the tropics—hues recall oranges, lemons, limes, and other fruits. We used color lavishly but judiciously throughout. For example, the kitchen cabinets are an exuberant lime green, and the tone of the window treatments and a custom Tibetan carpet in the living room remind us of a ripe mango.

Further details connect the house to Florida and the tropics in other ways. The foyer is clad in custom-carved keystone, a locally quarried oolitic limestone. We also took inspiration from the tropical bird aviaries that are a centerpiece of the Fisher Island Club in selecting the silk wall covering for the dining room. The kitchen walls are likewise covered in a material that evokes the tropics, natural grass cloth. The rear architectural panels of the dining room were antique finds discovered in nearby Miami Beach—they are of pine, and were given a new life here by being simply repainted and starched up for a more formal look. All the paintings in the house are by artists from Florida or Latin America.

A trip to the Paris Flea Market yielded some unique finds that, surprisingly, fit perfectly here as well and convey an established feeling, including a filigree wrought-iron grandfather clock and a pair of chandeliers that now grace the living room. We find something romantic and even fateful about using antiques that are found locally too, however. There is something special about a piece, like the French Art Deco buffet in the dining room, that may have traveled a long way in terms of both miles and time to be finally adopted in one of our local interiors. We always shop locally for antiques and market finds first.

In the foyer, right, the walls are lined with Florida keystone, while the parquet de Versailles–style floors are made of hand-scraped walnut. The center table dates to the 1940s, and tall-backed French chairs against the walls are upholstered in green silk. The wall sconces are from David Iatesta, and the vase is from Oggetti. PREVIOUS PAGE: The wrought-iron motif first encountered on the front doors is repeated on the adjacent foyer's stair rail.

An antique globe light fixture, above, that illuminates the foyer below and serves as a focal point in a second-story hall was found at Downtown in Los Angeles. The Louis XVII–style chairs are covered in vibrant tangerine silk. A pair of French canopy chairs, right, are covered in a print depicting tropical plants from Clarence House.

A coffee table featuring a palmetto leaf insert, above, was inspired by the work of T. H. Robsjohn-Gibbings and was hand-crafted in Miami by George Peace of Peace Millwork Company. A bronze chandelier with crystal netting, right, is a find from the Paris flea market. The painting above the Florida keystone mantel is by Gavin Perry. The silk area rug features a custom design that relates to the room's other gilt and reflective touches.

Vintage 1970s dinnerware and beaded wood napkin rings, above, adapt well to an exuberantly colored dining area. A white iron chandelier featuring plaster birds, right, brings some of the local fauna in, while the table below features an Italian banana bowl and vintage monkeys to complete the nod to the tropical location. PREVIOUS PAGES, LEFT: A brown wicker daybed sits on a terrace perfect for contemplating the view next to a bronze table with a monkey base. PREVIOUS PAGES, RIGHT: A De Simone fish sculpture from Italy adds color and humor to the poolside.

Brown, white, and orange tones unite patterns and form in an informal seating area, left and above. A sectional is upholstered in warm-weather-appropriate linen, a small console table sports an elephant motif, and wood shutters feature a geometric shape open enough to allow sunlight through. Botanical prints of seashells line the walls.

A dolphin fountain set into harlequin-pattern tile, above, calls to mind some of Florida's denizens. Marble surfaces in the master bathroom, right, provide a dramatic backdrop for vintage Art Deco wall sconces. The walls are surfaced in Calacatta gold and the wainscoting and counters are finished in a complementary green stone. PREVIOUS PAGES: Bronze herons decorate the house both indoors and out. OVERLEAF: Vegetal patterns help a bedroom relate to its richly verdant surroundings. Walls are covered in a printed linen from Osborne & Little, while vintage French beds upholstered in a tufted white show off linens with embroidered flower patterns. The blue-and-green glass light fixture was a junk store find.

traditional

Passing Time is the name our clients, football giant Dan Marino and his wife, Claire, gave this house. Though it's not in Florida, the house and its owners have strong roots in the Sunshine State. The Marinos are long-time Floridians; he was the quarterback for the Miami Dolphins from 1983 until 1999 and held or still has almost every passing record in pro football. They have been our clients for several decades, and each project we have worked on for them has achieved its own strong personality.

This is an oceanfront house on Kiawah Island—nestled between Charleston, South Carolina, and Savannah, Georgia. Like most of the "low-country" islands, Kiawah has a verdant natural beauty, and this particular house has a dramatic setting on a 500-foot-long boardwalk that looks down over the dunes to the Atlantic Ocean. You approach the house by driving down a 1000-foot-long, oak-shaded driveway.

The first task was to remodel this coastal, three-story, shingle-and-brick house. It was originally designed by Shope Reno Wharton Architects of Connecticut, and we worked with Zach T. Carney on the interiors. We opted for a look that was not a hackneyed or cliché adaptation of Southern stereotypes, but rather one that reflected the nautical, seaside setting.

The Marinos' primary wish was for more family space. They host large holiday celebrations and their grown children tend to come home for vacations—with friends in tow—so there's often a crowd. It's a big family and they "live large," so to gain space the verandas were enclosed and certain exterior walls and even fireplaces were removed. Those maneuvers essentially doubled the size of the first floor. With that extra square footage, we created a great room with a number of different seating areas, and inserted clerestory windows to ensure that natural light could permeate the space. Now part of the family can play games while others watch sports and still others can sit and chat. This main gathering area functions almost like a club room.

Particular attention is paid to the interior finishes, which include walnut floors and shellacked shingles in a stair hall that had originally been an exterior space. To further tie this house to its seaside, subtropical location, we used materials such as crushed oyster shell in the locally made countertops and grass cloth on the master bedroom walls.

The overall palette used in the home reflects its coastal setting as well, but in unexpected ways. Dan Marino specifically asked to include a lot of blue, so the great room relies on a color scheme based on blue, white, and brown. The patterns and materials chosen, however, are sophisticated and have strong references to history. The use of antiques strengthens allusions to the textiles and patterns brought to the West via the early silk and spice trade routes. On a practical note, the fabrics we used to upholster the furniture are all one hundred percent solution-dyed acrylic—at once beautiful and durable. Similarly, the living room carpet was custom-designed by us and woven by Amish craftsmen in Pennsylvania; its subtle but powerful presence and texture allude to the quality of Colonial craftsmanship found throughout neighboring Charleston.

We were lucky to find two antique, broken-pedestal-topped cabinets in a local antiques store that was going out of business—they proved perfect for showing off Dan's many football trophies. Ironically, they were the only pieces left in the store by the time we arrived. Elsewhere in the house, natural "trophies" from the ocean such as shells and coral fill shelves.

Our goal was to create a very personal family home that reflected a high level of taste. Striking a balance between livability and high style, however, is always a delicate balance, especially when houses receive a lot of foot traffic and are near an ocean and its lovely but corrosive elements. The finished house reflects its seaside location in subtle ways, but it also communicates some big ideas on how to live well in a boisterous crowd.

A rear view of the house, above. It was originally designed by Shope Reno Wharton Architects of South Norwalk, Connecticut. PREVIOUS PAGE: Subtle uses of tactile textiles and finishes impart a nautical mood. The rug at the landing is a cotton Dhurrie strip, and the stairs are covered in a runner of sisal with a navy binding. The bamboo settee is French, and is upholstered in Madagascar cloth. Bamboo mirrors hang above it on the walls, which were redone in tongue-in-groove wood paneling to impart a sense of warmth and familiarity.

Details such as an antique sailor's valentine, a Swedish Mora clock, an oyster-shell-encrusted mirror, blue-and-white decorative accents, and glass fishing floats, above, speak to the house's oceanside location. A rustic chandelier made of rope, iron, and wood, right, hangs over a round, custom-made walnut table. PREVIOUS PAGES: A custom-designed, braided rug ties together a room of blue-and-white accents. The ottoman is topped with a tray of cream leather and surrounded by sofas reupholstered in durable white indoor-outdoor fabric perfect for a beachside home.

Accents in deep tones add
contrast to a corner of the
great room. The ornately
carved cocktail table is
vintage Moroccan, a brass
football trophy stands on the
sill, and a barley-twist arm-
chair's frame adds texture.
Natural materials, such as
grass shades on the win-
dows and linen slipcovers,
complete the space in a
casual yet well-appointed
way. OVERLEAF: An outsized
pot rack from Ann-Morris
Antiques hints at the fact
that the house is used for
entertaining large crowds.
The grassy, reeded backs
of Orkney stools bring the
decorative use of natural
materials elsewhere in the
house into the kitchen as
well.

A collection of vintage brown-and-white transferware plates on a wall, above, all depict water scenes. The mosaic backsplash is intended to resemble oyster shells. Calacatta gold marble, used on the countertops, proved an ideal match for the space's other neutral-hued accents. An antique pine cabinet found in Charleston, right, displays some of Dan Marino's many football trophies.

Caning helps an English rosewood cabinet, above, relate to the nautical accents throughout the house while detailed carving on a French mirror from Brittany helps define the mood of a stair landing as formal. The decorative boxes are made from porcupine needles. To gain more living space, an exterior foyer, right, was enclosed and its shingles shellacked. The light fixtures are from Urban Electric of Charleston.

A bathroom, above, features mosaic floors, a marble shower, and a collection of decorative objects with a sea-going theme. OPPOSITE, CLOCKWISE FROM TOP LEFT: Moroccan pillows add flair to a bed. A club chair and its ottoman are upholstered in a bold brown-and-white stripe. Plants from the surrounding landscape inspired the use of vegetal patterns on the house's interior. The secretary was custom designed to fit the available space. PREVIOUS PAGES: A formal four-poster bed that dominates a master bedroom looks at home on a rug of abaca grass.

A director's chair, above, is a souvenir of Dan Marino's from his appearance in the movie *Ace Ventura: Pet Detective*. It sits next to an outdoor shower. A small dining area, right, looks out over the view to the Atlantic Ocean. PREVIOUS PAGES: Double chaises at poolside feature pillows with striped fabric sewn into concentric squares.

ACKNOWLEDGMENTS

The creation of this book is a dream come true for us and there are many to thank, not only for the publication itself, but for the creation of the work within its covers. Foremost we would like to thank our clients past and present for placing their trust in us. It is our fondest wish that you enjoy living in your homes as much as we enjoy creating them.

We want to acknowledge each other for the love and passion through the years that has sustained our enthusiasm not just for design, but for life itself. We also want to thank our children, Lauren and Jeremy, for being our most devoted fans throughout this journey.

The support of family and friends is one of the most important ingredients in any pursuit. We would like to thank my brother, Barry Gray, for his valued advice and also our friend Susan Richard, whose creative insight helped us close one door and open many others. We want to acknowledge Tom Murphy for being our greatest advocate, our toughest critic, and our good friend.

Our work has always been a collaborative exercise, and we consider ourselves fortunate to have had so many talented architects and designers on the Taylor & Taylor team, past and present. We owe a debt of gratitude to all our architects, starting with Keith Soto, Juan Carlos Menendez, and Howard Law, and continuing with Sandra Diaz, Daniel Gomez, Larry Seitz, and Fernando Torre-Sarlat. Thanks is also due to our interior designers Nancie Novak, Amber Thomas, Margarita Brito, and Alicja Sidorek. We want to thank Yvonne Enriquez for being such a mother hen, Tatiana Perez for answering to us all so cheerfully, and Jody Johnson, our business coach, whose guidance and wisdom we could not do without. We appreciate the contributions of Kevin Phillips, Carlotta Marks, and Charles Graff, whose attention to our details seem to make all the difference.

We extend our heartfelt thanks to everyone who played a part in the creation of this book: Peter Sallick and Keith Granet for including us; Tom Callaway for making a pivotal introduction; and Jill Cohen for believing in us and bringing us to The Monacelli Press. We are grateful to Stacee Lawrence, our editor, for her expertise and guidance, and to Doug Turshen for his artful layouts. Thank you Debra Whitlaw Llewellyn and Chris Pinel for the beautiful images contained in this book, and thank you, Beth Dunlop, for listening so well and for writing even better.

CREDITS

NAUTICAL
Architectural Renovation: Taylor & Taylor
Interior Design: Taylor & Taylor
Landscape Architect: General Landscaping
Builder: North South Construction
Craftsman: Peace Millwork

CLASSICAL
Architecture: Taylor & Taylor
Interior Design: Taylor & Taylor
Landscape Architect: Sanchez & Maddox
Builder: Coastal Homes
Craftsmen: Merrit Millwork, Hardwood Design Flooring, Marble Crafters, G Metals, Workroom for Designers

MEMORABLE
Architecture: Taylor & Taylor
Interior Design: Taylor & Taylor
Landscape Architect: Scott Redmond
Builder: Ray Coudriet

ENVIRONMENTAL
Architecture: Duany Plater-Zyberk & Co.; Elizabeth Plater-Zyberk with Christina Miller
Architect of Record: Jorge Esteban, AIA
Interior Architecture: Taylor & Taylor
Interior Design: Taylor & Taylor
Landscape Architect: Geomantic Designs Robert Parsley
Builder: Coastal Homes
LEED Consultants: Spinnaker Group
Craftsmen: Matrix Z Seastone, Escobar Millwork, Nanze Hardware, Larry's Cap & Stone, Le Jeune Upholstery

PERSONAL
Architecture: Taylor & Taylor
Interior Design: Taylor & Taylor
Builder: Lowell Homes
Craftsmen: Hardwood Design Flooring, G Metal, Calhoun & Sons Plasterwork, Keystone Creations, Peace Millwork

MONUMENTAL
Architecture: Cooper Johnson Smith with Don Cooper
Interior Architecture: Taylor & Taylor
Interior Design: Taylor & Taylor
Builder: Alvarez Homes
Landscape Architect: Ted Kempton
Craftsmen: Splatt Paint, AlliKriste Fine Cabinetry & Kitchen Design, Draper-DBS

HISTORICAL
Architecture: Taylor & Taylor
Interior Architecture: Taylor & Taylor
Interior Design: Taylor & Taylor
Landscape Architecture: Sanchez & Maddox

Builder: The Marker Group
Craftsmen: Merrit Millwork, Escobar Millwork, Marble Crafters, Foster Reeve & Assoc. Plasterworks

PERENNIAL
Architecture: Taylor & Taylor
Interior Design: Doug Griewe
Landscape Architecture: Don Trezona
Builder: Stathis Construction

TROPICAL
Architect of Record: Tom Benedict
Interior Architecture: Taylor & Taylor
Interior Design: Taylor & Taylor
Landscape Architecture: Hall & Aqui
Builder: Coastal Homes
Craftsmen: Akouri Metalworks, Hardwood Designs Flooring, Viking Millwork, Keystone Creations

TRADITIONAL
Architect: Shope Reno Wharton
Renovation Architect: Zach T. Carney
Architecture with James Selvitelli
Interior Architecture: Taylor & Taylor
Interior Design: Taylor & Taylor
Builder: Sifly Homes, Inc.
Craftsmen: Absolute Hardwood Flooring, Le Jeune Upholstery

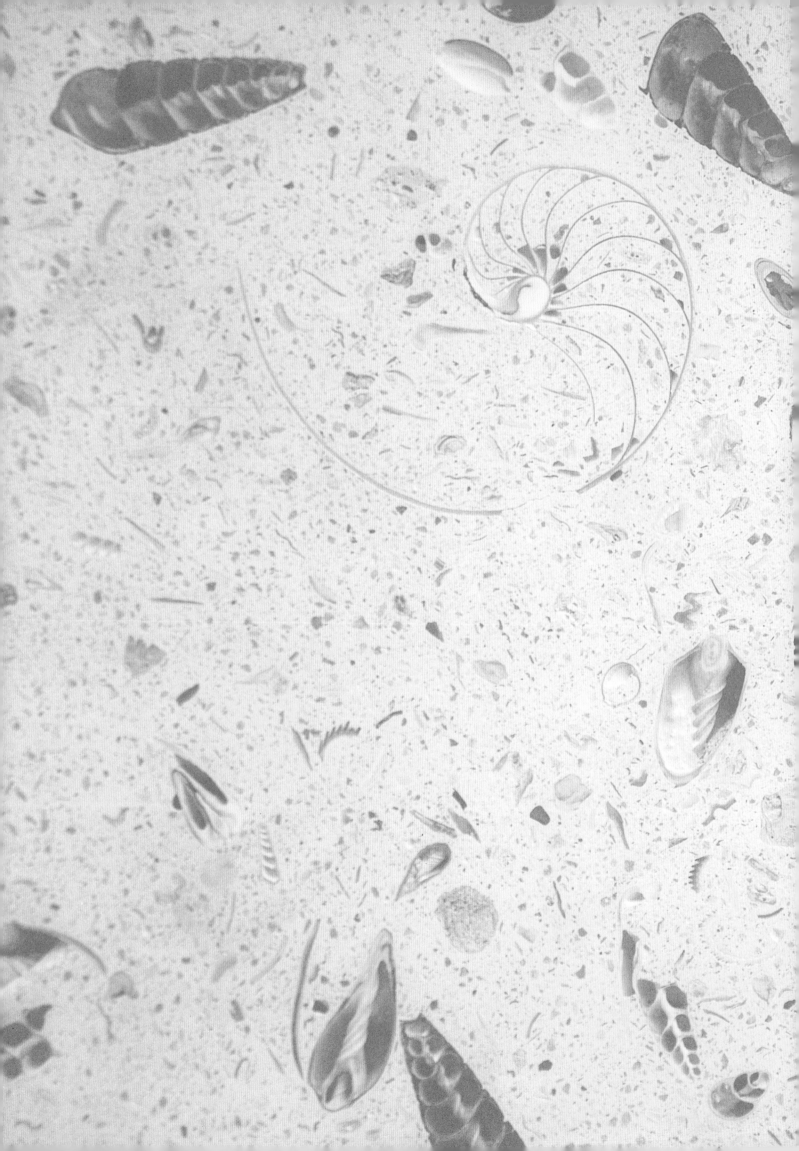